# The **Wubbulous** Gallery to **Color**

illustrated by Segundo Garcia

Random House / Jim Henson Productions, Inc.

Based on the television series *The Wubbulous World of Dr. Seuss*™, produced by Jim Henson Productions, Inc.

**The Cat in the Hat
and
Little Cats A, B, and C**

**The Mullally Family**

**The Mullally Family (continued)**

**Horton the Elephant**

**Thidwick & Friends**

**The Grinch in his Grotto**

**The Zubble-wump Hatches!**

**The Zubble-wump, Free at Last!**

**His Majesty, King Lindy**

**His Majesty, King Noogle**

**Elwood the Jester**

**The Royal Barbering Barbarians**

**The Royal Pretender**

**Elwood and Princess Mindy**

**The Royal Brothers Reunited**

**Former Trusted Adviser, Yertle the Turtle**

**The Wickersham Brothers**

**Fox and Mr. Knox**

**The Dorfmans**

**The Gink**

**Eliza and her Beloved Pet**

**The Gink and Company**

**Horton the Explorer and Gink Authority**

**Tiddlyginks**

**Little Gink, Happy at Last!**

**Hats, Hats, and More Hats!**

**Susan Bocks Dutter Docks Berklummer Snue**

**Sue Snue and
Uncles Docks, Berklummer,
and Dutter**

**Cats A, B, and C**

**Horton Has a Hit**

**Horton and Morton**

**Norval at Home**

**It's a Wubbulous World!**

**The Simplifier**

**Mrs. Zabarelli**

**Mrs. Zabarelli's Band**

**The Cat on Vacation**

**Horton the Bellhop**

**The Grinch Departs**